Akbar

Gomathi Krishnan

Prodigy

Akbar
Gomathi Krishnan ©

First Edition: January 2008
56 Pages
Printed in India.

ISBN 978-81-8368-658-7
Pro-ya-en - 9

Prodigy Books
177/103, First Floor, Ambal's Building
Lloyds Road, Royapettah, Chennai 600 014.
Ph: +91-44-4200-9603
Email: support@nhm.in
Website: www.nhm.in

Prodigy Books is an imprint of New Horizon Media Pvt. Ltd.

In the middle of a fierce battle, the news of the birth of a son was relayed to the king. Humayun's happiness knew no bounds. The delighted king exclaimed, 'Praise to Allah! I have been blessed with a son and heir to my throne. I name this son of mine—born to be the greatest of kings—'Akbar'.'

Humayun's period of happiness was, however, short-lived as he driven into exile to Persia. He was forced to leave his 14-month-old son, Akbar, in Kandahar under the protection of his uncle, Askari.

Introduction

India, as we all know, is a land of many languages, religions, and cultures. She has welcomed people from different parts of the world and embraced them as her own children.

Among the many conquerors of India, the most prominent were the Mughals who left behind a magnificent legacy. In fact, they left their mark on almost every aspect of day-to-day life.

The Mughals were the descendants of the Mongols—Central Asian nomads—in particular the Mongol warriors of Genghis Khan. The word 'Mughal' is the Persian equivalent of 'Mongol'.

The Mughals spread their Persian culture throughout India through a series of conquests. They firmly believed in Islam and its mystical doctrine of a Divine Light which they referred to as the Imam—a religious guide on earth. The Mughals also believed in Sufi mysticism, a branch of Islam that emphasised the union of man with God.

The Mughals are remembered today for their deep involvement in arts, culture and architecture. Their architectural excellence is evident from the monumental splendours they have left behind. Apart from their interest in cultural pursuits, the Mughals were also well known for their political intelligence. The Mughal rulers were just and united a number of provinces under one rule—something that the previous invaders and Indian kings had failed to achieve.

The Mughal dynasty in India can be traced to the early 16th century. It began with the reign of Babur in the 1520s and more or less ended with Aurangzeb in the early 1700s. A few minor Mughal kings ruled after Aurangzeb, but were not as prominent as their predecessors.

Of all the Mughal emperors who ruled India, Akbar was the most renowned. This book will tell you about this benevolent and charismatic king who won the hearts of many through his kindness and valour. He was rightly called 'Akbar the Great'.

The Early Mughals

Babur (1483 – 1530)

Zahiruddin Muhammad, better known as Babur, was born on February 14, 1483, in the town of Andijan, Fergana Valley—present day Uzbekistan. Babur hailed from the Barlas tribe which was of Mongol origin, but his tribe also embraced Turkic and Persian cultures and converted to Islam. They settled in Turkestan and Khorasan. They spoke the Chaghatai language—known to Babur and his clan as 'Turkish'. Babur was equally at home in Persian and the lingua franca of the Timurid elite. His famous work, the *Baburnama*, was written in Turkish.

At the age of twelve, Babur succeeded his father, much to the resentment of his relatives. Babur conquered Kabul in 1504 and assumed the title 'Badshah'. Between 1504 and 1510, Babur concentrated on building his army and was also engaged in cultural activities.

There was no looking back for Babur after the conquest of Fergana and Samarkhand in 1510. He acquired territory after territory, following in the footsteps of his ancestor Genghis Khan.

The Mughal Empire took root in the early 15th century in Kabul and the eastern regions of Khorasan. Slowly but steadily, Babur spread the reach of his realm across the fertile region of Sind and the lower valley of the Indus River. Three major battles made him the all powerful ruler of Northern India. These were the Battle of Panipat, the Battle of Khanwa and the Battle of Ghaghra.

The First Battle of Panipat (1526)

In 1526, Babur defeated Ibrahim Lodhi the ruler of the Delhi Sultanate. The small village of Panipat, in present day Haryana, became the battlefield. Babur's use of gunpowder, firearms and field artillery caused the downfall of Lodhi, whose army was not equipped with such ammunition. Babur's guns scared the elephants, which trampled Lodhi's men. Lodhi was abandoned by his men to die all alone in the battle field.

The Battle of Khanwa (1527)

Following the Battle of Panipat, Babur fought against Rana Sanga of Mewar. This battle was fought on 17 March 1572, near the village of Khanwa, about 60 km west of Agra. Rana Sanga, formally known as Maharana Sangram Singh I, ruled Mewar before he was defeated in the war. Babur's forces were outnumbered by the forces of Rana Sanga but, once again, it was Babur's artillery that gave him an edge over his opponents.

The Battle of Ghaghra (1529)

The third and final battle was the Battle of Ghaghra. This was fought near Varanasi, in present day Uttar Pradesh, on 6 May 1529, between Babur and Mahmud Lodhi—the brother of Ibrahim Lodhi. Babur's victory over Mahmud Lodhi crushed all resistance to Babur's supremacy and firmly established the Mughal Empire in the northern part of the Indian subcontinent.

Early Mughal architecture

Apart from being a fierce warrior, Babur had a great sense of beauty. He travelled extensively and was greatly inspired by the beautiful landscapes he came across. He built a series of structures displaying the carved patterns of Hindu architecture. He also balanced Persian and Hindu architectural techniques and the result was a treat to the eyes.

Babur died at the age of 48 and was buried in a mausoleum in Agra which went against his wish to be buried in Kabul. Nine years after his death, Sher Shah Suri fulfilled Babur's dream by burying him in a beautiful garden called Bagh-e-Babur in Kabul.

Humayun (1508 – 1556)

Nasiruddin Humayun, a son of Emperor Babur, became the second Mughal emperor of India in 1530. Humayun lost his kingdom soon after he ascended the throne. After his initial series of defeats, Humayun fled to Persia with his wife Hamida. After years of exile, with Persian aid and the wise decision to use Bairam Khan's military skills, Humayun captured Punjab and other places in the Northern provinces. With Sher Shah's death, Delhi was easily seized. Humayun invaded many neighbouring parts of Delhi and finally ascended the throne in Delhi on 15 July 1555. During his period he ruled over Afghanistan, Pakistan and parts of northern India.

Humayun was superstitious and interested in astrology and the occult. Driven by his interests, he devised a form of administration based on the four elements—earth for agriculture and agricultural sciences; fire for the military; water for canals and waterways; and air for the rest of life's activities. It is said that he organised his daily routine based on the planetary motions of the day.

Humayun was deeply inspired by Persian ways of living. He also adopted the military techniques which he observed in Persia. He followed the Persian methods of governance with great success. He loved astronomy and built many observatories in his state. He encouraged artists and appointed many painters in his court. Humayun's architectural masterpiece was the city of Din-Panah built at the start of his reign but this city was razed to the ground by Sher Shah Suri.

Humayun's interest in the arts led to the creation of some exquisite paintings. He also encouraged many literary talents in his court. His life was chronicled in a work called the *Humayunnama* written by his sister Gulbadan Begum. Six months after he became king, Humayun fell down his library stairs. The fall was fatal.

Akbar – the Young Prince

Jalaluddin Muhammad Akbar (1542– 1605), son of Humayun, succeeded his father at the age of 13. Akbar was forced to ascend the throne after Humayun's accidental death.

Akbar was born in Sindh where Humayun and his 15-year-old wife, Hamida, were staying as refugees. Humayun was, at that time, fighting against Sindh. Soon after this he was forced into exile. Humayun fled Umarkot with Hamida leaving the 14-month-old Akbar under the care of Askari, Humayun's brother. Akbar spent the first few years of his life with his uncle in the rough terrains of Afghanistan.

Akbar was the only Mughal king to have remained uneducated, a strange fact among the Mughals who were famous for their excellence in learning. Akbar's lack of education came about because of his stay in his uncle's home. He was deprived of normal schooling and denied a personal tutor to teach him the alphabet. While his grandfather and father were accomplished scholars, Akbar grew up illiterate.

Askari's reason for denying his nephew his basic rights was perhaps the hatred he had towards his brother, Humayun. Humayun, a dreamer, was his father's favourite son and Babur had ensured that he was made heir to the throne. So, it was but natural that when Akbar was entrusted into his custody, Askari found solace in depriving the young prince of his basic right to education.

Humayun returned victorious with the aid of Persian troops a few years later. The dreamer in him gone, Humayun came back a refined man—with a warrior's spirit. In the days that followed, Humayun regained all the land he had lost, including his father's dreamland—Kabul.

Akbar, after being reunited with his parents, was put under the tutelage of the able General Bairam Khan. Akbar was considered to be most princely in his manners even from a very young age. He was a born sportsman and an expert hunter. His physical power and his daring caused even the fiercest of troops to surrender. Despite these qualities in the young king, Bairam Khan was made his guardian on the death of Humayun. So the rule of Bairam Khan prevailed until Akbar came of age.

Bairam Khan

Bairam Khan was an Iranian noble who served both Humayun and Akbar. He was a major force in rebuilding the Mughal Empire in India after Babur's kingdom fell apart. He was born in Badakhshan and belonged to the Baharlu clan of the Turkmen tribe. His ancestors had ruled Western Persia for centuries before being overthrown by the Safavid dynasty.

Bairam Khan helped Humayun win many a battle and then ruled the Mughal Empire until Akbar came of age. He was known for his excellence in military skills and literary pursuits.

Bairam Khan was a strict disciplinarian who kept the pretenders to the throne at bay. He was responsible for the expansion of the Mughal territory in the initial years of Akbar's rule. He ensured that power was centralised and maintained order in the provinces. Bairam Khan had many rivals who were constantly plotting against him. The main opposition to Bairam Khan's came from Akbar's aunt, Maham Anga and her son, Adham Khan. But his dedication to the royal throne made him ignore all these minor obstacles. Bairam Khan's major achievement under the reign of Akbar was the second battle of Panipat. It was Khan who urged Akbar to wage war against Hemu to re-conquer Delhi. This battle established the Mughal rule in the northern province of India once again. What Humayun had lost in his lifetime, and much more, was regained and captured by Akbar and Bairam Khan, within the first few days of his coronation.

When Akbar turned 18, he asked Bairam Khan to step down as regent and go on a pilgrimage to Mecca. Hurt, Bairam Khan chose to rebel against the king but he was defeated and imprisoned. However, the closeness between him and Akbar overcame their enmity. Akbar forgave him and offered to give him back his post. Bairam Khan declined and set off for Mecca. On the way, he was murdered.

Maham Anga and Adham Khan

Maham Anga, Akbar's nurse, was one of the aspirants to his throne. After Bairam Khan's dismissal in 1560, Maham Anga tried to keep Akbar as a puppet ruler. Her attempts were, however unsuccessful, for Akbar had a mind of his own even at a very young age.

Adham Khan, Akbar's foster brother and Maham Anga's son, was a general in Akbar's army. He was an arrogant young man whose cruelty was known throughout the province. Akbar gave him many opportunities to reform himself, but Adham Khan did not change. He crossed the limits of decency when Akbar sent him to capture Malwa in 1561, following the death of Bairam Khan.

Malwa's ruler, Baz Bahadur, was a talented musician, but had no capacity to rule a kingdom. Hearing of the approaching Mughal force, Baz Bahadur fled, leaving behind his wives and his kingdom. Adham Khan took advantage of this and abused the captive women in a terrible manner.

When Akbar heard of his foster brother's misdeeds he was enraged. He went personally to take charge of Malwa. Adham Khan, fearing punishment, begged for forgiveness. Akbar did forgive him, but when he found out that Adham Khan had hidden two of the women for himself he was livid. Maham Anga killed both the women, lest they reveal her son's cruelty to the King. Akbar was left with no other choice but to assume complete control over his kingdom. In 1562, he took absolute charge and appointed Atkah Khan as his Prime Minister.

Adham Khan, unwilling to accept his foster brother's decision, picked up a fight with Atkah Khan and stabbed him. He also entered the royal women's quarters and caused trouble there. Akbar rushed to the spot only to find his prime minister in a pool of blood. Things went completely out of hand when Adham Khan laid a hand on Akbar's shoulder—a clear sign of disrespect towards the elder brother in Islamic culture. Akbar punched Adham on his face, making him unconscious. He then ordered his men to throw him over the parapet. It is believed that Akbar himself conveyed the news of Adham Khan's death to Maham Anga. She did not survive long after that.

The 19-year-old Akbar assumed complete power over his empire after this incident. Akbar was a daring man, always ready to risk his life to defend the empire. His subjects were well respected and honoured according to their merits. Akbar loved his relatives and was always kind to them—except on rare occasions when he felt compelled to punish them severely, as in the case of Adham Khan.

Akbar – the Mughal Emperor

Akbar was a wise ruler with innovative ideas. He was also a sound judge of character. Under his rule, many changes were introduced in the administration of the provinces. His ideas on land reforms and his views on religion were unique.

Akbar did not believe in being content with the area he was governing. He expanded his kingdom all through his life—Malwa, Gujarat, Bengal, Kabul, Kashmir, Kandesh and many other neighbouring provinces. For each province he appointed a trustworthy governor who worked under his direct authority. This helped him keep a close check on any uprising against him.

Akbar did not want to settle in Delhi and as a result moved his court to Fatehpur Sikri, near Agra. He soon found this arrangement unprofitable and set up a roaming camp that helped him to be near all his provinces.

Akbar was born during great political unrest and was a witness to his parents' exile at a very young age. He saw his father's political errors and realised the necessity for ideal rule in India. He was fully aware of the importance of a firmly grounded dynasty and resolved to establish one in India. He also vowed at an early age that when the Mughals returned to India, it would be to stay forever.

Being deprived of princely comforts in his early childhood, Akbar learnt the realities of life. This made him a better king for he was able to fully understand and empathise with his subjects. It was this understanding that helped him formulate rules and enact reformation that bettered the lives of his people. His subjects lived in prosperity and harmony.

Unlike Humayun and even Babur, Akbar saw the flaws in the early Mughal administration. He understood that if a successful empire was to be established, it would be necessary to let go of the traditional form of governance. A number of administrative reforms were thus introduced during his reign.

Islamic law gave the ruler of the state absolute power over the people, irrespective of their religion. This traditional method of rule was the first to be abolished by Akbar. He saw the traditional method as the main obstacle in his path to achieving total confidence from his subjects, the majority of whom were non-Muslims.

Babur, the first Mughal ruler, was not tolerant of other religious beliefs. He did not allow freedom of worship for other religious groups. This policy of religious intolerance was followed till Akbar came to power. Contrary to his predecessors, Akbar encouraged people from other religious groups to actively participate in the state's politics and also encouraged them to become members of his court.

He entered into matrimonial alliances with the Rajput royal families. Akbar married the princess of Amber, Hira Kumari, who later took the name Jodhabai. She was the mother of Prince Salim, better known as Jahangir. Akbar married many Rajput princesses and also a Christian lady. He firmly believed that these inter-religious marriages would bring people of various faiths closer and help establish peaceful co-existence. The extent of peaceful co-existence he achieved is debatable, but what he definitely achieved through these alliances was the support and service of the Rajputs for the next 100 years.

Akbar's Court

Mansandars and zamindars

Akbar had to wage many battles to acquire his vast empire. To avoid making enemies of the kings he conquered he introduced the method of incorporation, that is, he made them zamindars or mansandars of the provinces that they had lost in battle to him. This gave them the power to exercise their rule over their subjects as before and also gave them the satisfaction of being rulers. Akbar's sole demand was that they accept his superiority and be loyal to him, a condition to which the vanquished kings readily agreed. The policy of incorporation helped him delegate the running of these small towns and villages to the rulers themselves. This also gave him time to concentrate on expanding his empire.

In order to maintain continued loyalty from his subjects, Akbar had to create a system by which they would feel part of the throne. Akbar introduced many measures to bring this about.

Akbar's court

1. He introduced the ritual of a daily assembly in which he was present.
2. He gave his subjects and his subordinate kings the sense of legitimacy through display of power by firmly establishing his sovereignty.
3. Akbar saw to it that the local officials accepted his absolute rule which in turn made the people accept him.
4. In court, he followed both Hindu and Muslim rites which made him popular with both the religious groups.
5. A few of his famous ritual practices were: jharuka—appearing in the balcony to present himself to the public each morning; tuladan—distribution of gifts equivalent to his weight on auspicious occasions and, most important of all, was the daily public gathering in Diwan-I-Aam.
6. Tiny portraits of Akbar were issued to all his officials who wore them on their turbans as a mark of acceptance of his rule.

Akbar believed that his appearing in front of the public was not only a show of power but also assured his subjects of the stability of his empire. Given his rapidly expanding empire and the fast growing trade and commerce across his kingdom, Akbar had to be on the alert to prevent any malicious news from spreading among his subjects. These cautious acts nipped in the bud any form of uprising.

The glory of the Mughal Empire rested to a fair extent on the harmonious relationship between Akbar and his subjects.

Apart from this, Akbar maintained personal ties with each of his officials. These officials served in the imperial court for at least one month during their tenure. Akbar discussed possible improvements to the administration and state affairs with them at great length.

During their time at court, the officials experienced the grandeur of their emperor and his court and also learnt proper court etiquette. While at the imperial court, they were also required to perform guard duty for a week and participate in all court rituals. Akbar always bestowed gifts on his officials when they were in his court and, when they were away in their provinces, he sent them gifts through messengers.

In course of time, Akbar obtained the loyalty of his officials and they became walking signifiers of Akbar himself throughout the empire. The objective of affirming the glory of the empire to all its subjects was also achieved through the incorporation policy and royal rituals brought in by Akbar.

His Reforms

Land revenue system

The most noteworthy achievement of Akbar was his tax reform policy. His wise agricultural moves improved the produce of crops in his kingdom. His successful implementation of this policy enhanced the Mughal Empire's wealth for future generations. This system of land tax was considered to be a distinct improvement from the earlier systems of the Egyptians and the Romans. This reform system is believed to have been first implemented by the famous Chinese king Kang Xi and it is said he achieved success just like Akbar did.

In order to gain a complete understanding of the land value and its productivity, Akbar instructed his officials to prepare a detailed and accurate land register. All land holdings were reclassified into five categories based on the fertility rate of the soil. A detailed report gave a clear picture of the soil quality, types of crops suited for each soil and water accessibility in different regions. This method of land tax stimulated the investment plans and enhanced the productive use of the land.

Based on the reports, Akbar and his advisers formulated a tax revenue system by establishing twelve provinces. Each of these provinces had its own administrative system with seven posts that functioned directly under the central power—Akbar. Akbar clearly differentiated between civil and military authority. He restricted to a great degree the autonomy of the provincial governors.

Military reforms

Prior to Akbar's reign, the armed forces did not enjoy any special benefits. They were soldiers with neither special ranks nor distinctions. They were also paid only during the time of war. During the days of peace, these soldiers were forced to take up odd jobs to feed themselves and their families. When Akbar ascended the throne he saw the sorry state of his armed forces and resolved to improve their lifestyle.

Akbar fought several battles in his lifetime. He was an excellent warrior but deemed it essential that his warriors be as valiant as he was. He introduced a series of reforms for his military forces. The reforms he introduced were:

1. The soldiers were ranked or grouped under different sections based on their fighting skills.
2. Each section was assigned duties depending on the degree of performance and capabilities.

3. All soldiers reported to the heads of their respective sections who in turn reported to the senior officer or general who headed the army. This general reported to the king.
4. The soldiers and their families were paid on a monthly basis.
5. The family members were also provided with jobs in the government based on their merits.
6. The soldiers were given proper training and new military strategies were developed.
7. The soldiers were suitably rewarded for their excellence in the battlefield.

This systematic organisation of the military sector enhanced the probability of their victory in the battlefield. It also helped the soldiers to perfect their fighting skills.

Other reforms

Akbar introduced several changes in the society to better the lives of his people. Among them, the reforms he formulated for women need special mention. Contrary to the patriarchal and conservative era he was born in, Akbar respected and believed in the equality of men and women. To support his belief he:

1. encouraged widow remarriage
2. condemned child marriage
3. outlawed the practice of sati
4. introduced primary education for girls

5. organised special market days for women

The reforms introduced by Akbar generated a hierarchy of officials with exclusive loyalty to the supreme power. This system was strictly against any religious aristocracy. Before the reign of Akbar, the Mughal court had high ranking officials taken only from the Islamic community. However, Akbar ended this practice by selecting men on the basis of merit. This brought to his court men from various religious backgrounds. The practice of religious tolerance gained Akbar recognition and appreciation from his subjects and established the reputation of the Mughal Empire as a place where all sujects were equal.

Akbar's Conquests

When Akbar ascended the throne there were constant threats of aggression from the neighbouring states. Though, Humayun had left behind a vast empire, Akbar had to fight to keep it. Most of his rivals did not take him seriously for he was only thirteen years old when he became king. Akbar, following the tradition of his ancestors, believed in conquering vast areas and centralising the Mughal power. To achieve this he had to wage several battles.

The Second Battle of Panipat

Akbar was crowned king of the Mughal Empire on 14 February 1556. At the time, the Mughal Empire was limited to only Kabul, Kandahar, and parts of Punjab and Delhi. Akbar had resolved to follow the example of his grandfather and the Timur clan and expand his territory as quickly and as constantly as possible.

Hemu, the prime minister of Muhammad Adil Shah Suri, slowly advanced against the Mughals. Hemu had established himself at Chunar as king of the region. Taking advantage of Humayun's

Areas ruled by Akbar

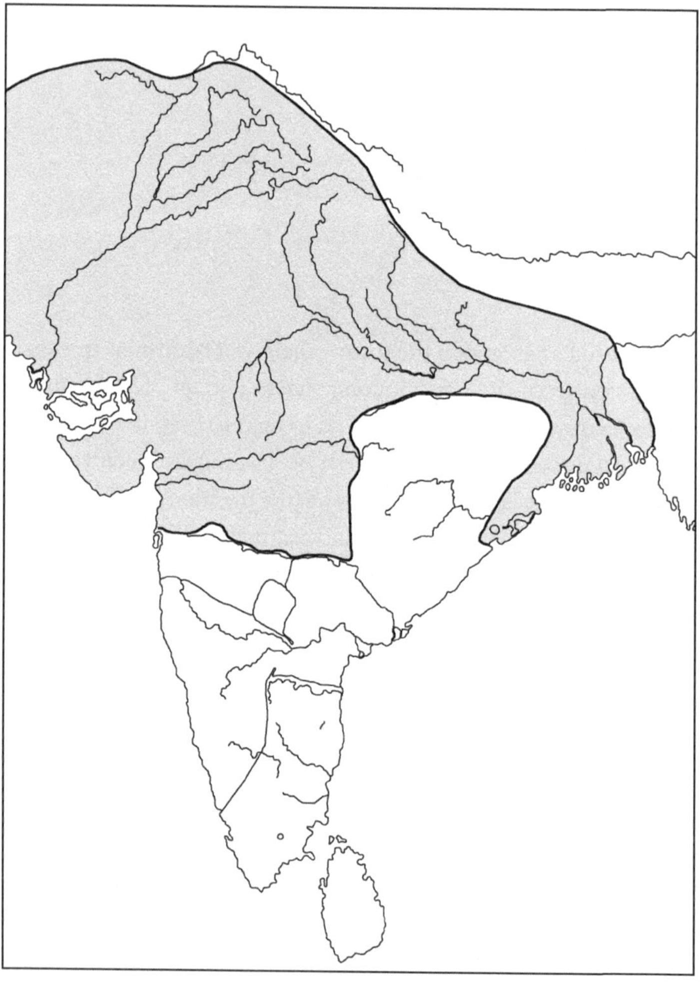

death, he wanted to expel the Mughals from India. He had managed to conquer Agra and Delhi and posed a great threat to Akbar's rule.

The enraged Bairam Khan urged Akbar to confront Hemu and led the Mughal army in a counter attack against him. This historic battle took place fifty miles north of Delhi on 5 November 1556. Hemu was almost winning the battle when a stray arrow struck him in the eye and rendered him unconscious. This ill luck caused panic among Hemu's soldiers. Hemu was brought unconscious before Akbar and Bairam Khan. Akbar touched Hemu's head with his sword according to the royal tradition and his associates beheaded him later. Akbar had Hemu's head sent to Kabul as a sign of his victory. The Mughals' sudden stroke of luck was unexpected, but nevertheless it firmly established Mughal rule in India for the next few centuries.

The Battle of Chittoor

Akbar conquered areas not only through battles but also by marrying into the ruling houses of various provinces. He married many Rajput princesses on the eastern front of the Rajputana Empire but he could never breach the kingdom of the supreme power of Rajasthan—the Rana of Mewar.

Uday Singh, the Rana of Mewar, unlike his weaker Rajput brothers, refused any alliance—personal or official—with the Mughals. This defiance posed a great challenge to the Mughals and infuriated Akbar who decided to wage war against Chittoor.

Uday Singh's armies were no match for the vast and powerful force of the Mughal king.

Seeing that defeat was imminent, Uday Singh handed the great fort of Chittoor into the care of his able commander Jai Mal. He then fled with his family to take refuge in the safety of the surrounding hills.

Akbar's vast army stretched over ten miles and in 1567 laid siege to the fort of Chittoor. The 8,000 Rajput soldiers under the commandership of Jai Mal guarded the fort against the Mughals.

Akbar had two strategies to win over the fort—mining and building a sabat. A sabat was a high wall structure that provided cover for the army as it advanced towards the enemy inch by inch. This structure moved almost unnoticed and finally surrounded the fort on all four sides. This left the enemy no way to escape; they could either die or surrender.

Akbar's idea of mining proved fatal to his own army. A missile that went off before time claimed the lives of 200 of his soldiers. A few more Mughal soldiers were lost to muskets fired from inside the fort. Enraged by this loss, Akbar led a fierce battle and after four months of severe warfare, Jai Mal was shot by Akbar's musket fire.

The death of their commander left the Rajputs with no leader. To escape the shame of capture and in keeping with the Rajput tradition of not surrendering to their enemies, thousands of

Rajput women performed jauhar—the act of self-immolation.

Following this Patta Singh, a young Rajput leader, along with a small army fought against the Mughal troops. They were soon defeated and the victorious Mughal army entered the fort of Chittoor. Akbar captured the fort with nearly 40, 000 Hindu peasants and hundreds of artisans. He ordered a massacre of all the Rajputs, though many of them escaped. This uncharacteristic act left a blot on Akbar's reputation.

Akbar wins Gujarat

Gujarat was an important centre of business in those days and Akbar realised its worth to his empire. In 1572, he started out to defeat the King of Gujarat, Muzaffar Shah III.

On 26 February 1573, Akbar captured Surat and led his army towards Ahmedabad which was an easy catch for a warrior like Akbar. On 2 September 1573 he conquered Ahmedabad and Gujarat became an integral part of the Mughal Empire.

Akbar's battle against Mirza Muhammad Hakim

Mirza Muhammad Hakim ruled over Kabul and was the half-brother of Akbar. Mirza was jealous of Akbar's vast empire and hatched a conspiracy against him. He joined hands with a few nobles from the eastern provinces and a few high ranking officers to usurp Akbar's throne. Mirza, according to the conspiracy, invaded Punjab in order to gain easier access to the throne of Hindustan.

Akbar, who had until then been extremely tolerant with his half-brother, could not take his insolence any more. He felt it necessary to teach his half-brother a good lesson and decided to wage war against him. On 8 February 1581, Akbar along with 500 war elephants and 50, 000 cavalry marched against Afghanistan.

Mirza did not expect this sudden outburst of anger from his brother. He was scared for he was well aware that he could never win against Akbar's mighty forces. He therefore fled and took refuge in Kabul.

On 9 August 1581, Akbar led his troops into Kabul and defeated Mirza Muhammad Hakim. The defeated Mirza begged for forgiveness and pledged his lifelong submission to Akbar. Akbar's anger had somewhat lessened and he reconciled with Mirza by restoring Kabul to his care. Kabul was later annexed to the Mughal Empire after the death of Mirza in 1585.

Through battles, personal alliances and by instilling fear, Akbar expanded his empire to vast areas. He was known for his military strategies, excellent administrative capabilities and courage to face the fiercest armies in the battlefield.

Akbar's Views on Religion

At the start of Akbar's reign, the majority of the high-ranking officials were Muslim. The emperor, with his radical views, was against such a monopoly and appointed non-Muslims in senior positions in his government. He fostered great tolerance for all religions. He went a step further by abolishing the pilgrim tax in the eighth year and the jizyah tax—tax levied on non-Muslims—in the ninth year of his reign.

Akbar was highly influenced by his Mongol heritage. From Genghis Khan he adopted the theory of the divine rule of the king. Through this theory he also learnt the importance of centralising the sovereign power and showing tolerance to all religions.

Akbar enjoyed a cordial relationship with the Roman Catholic Church which regularly sent Jesuit priests to his court for religious and intellectual discussions. He involved scholars from different faiths in such discussions. He did his best to remove all distinctions between Muslims and non-Muslims.

Akbar was an uneducated king, but this did not limit his wisdom. From the discussions held in his court, Akbar understood that no religion could claim the monopoly of truth. This inspired him to create a new religion, Din-i-Ilahi ('Divine Faith'), which aimed at merging the best aspects of Hinduism, Islam, Christianity, Jainism and Zoroastrianism. Through this new faith, he aimed to unite his subjects and remove the differences that prevailed among them.

Akbar built the Ibadat Khana ('Hall of Worship') at Fatehpur Sikri as a place where philosophical and religious issues could be debated. Din-i-Ilahi was a combination of mysticism, philosophy and nature worship. It did not identify gods or prophets. Many of his Muslim courtiers condemned this new faith as blasphemy. This religion had very few followers during the reign of Akbar and died a natural death after his demise. Other than Akbar, the only other followers of the Din-i-Ilahi were Birbal and Raja Man Singh, both of whom served in high positions in Akbar's court.

Akbar retained the Mughal doctrine of the divine mandate to rule, but changed the Timurid stance on conforming to Islamic standards. Akbar furthered the existing Muslim theory that the sultan was the shadow of God on earth. He claimed that his mandate to rule was God-given and that he had a sovereign nature that emanated from God. This two-fold doctrine of kingship elevated Akbar above all people and legitimised the Mughal lineage as eternally sovereign.

He brought about communal harmony through marriages

between followers of different religions and also through talks and discussions conducted in the Ibadat Khana. Many condemned his radical actions and said he was motivated by political considerations. But, no matter what was said about him, Akbar was truly committed to the cause of dissolving differences among his subjects and bringing unity to his empire.

Akbar's Architectural Excellence

That Akbar was a skilled architect is evident from the buildings still present within the premises of the Agra fort and the city of Fatehpur Sikri.

Fatehpur Sikri

The buildings in this imperial city belong to a composite style of architecture with a predominant Islamic style brilliantly merged with Rajasthani and Gujarati styles. The palaces in Fatehpur Sikri have ornate columns, extensive jali work, stone carvings and surface ornamentation. These palaces comprise rectangular courtyards with tiers of airy pavilions.

breeze. Through the screens the ladies could see a splendid view of the town. In the courtyard of the Panch Mahal, Akbar had a huge square-shaped area marked out as a board game called 'pachisi'. Dancing girls acted as live counters for the game!

Panch Mahal

Buland Darwaza

Diwan-i-Aam

The hall of public audience or Diwan-i-Aam appears near the entrance of Sikri. It is a huge rectangular walled-in courtyard with a royal balcony fitted with jali screens. Near the throne, Akbar's pet elephant, Hiran, was kept tied to a hook. According to legend, Hiran crushed the heads of the guilty underfoot but if he refused, the accused were let free.

Diwan-i-Khas

This lies enclosed behind the Diwan-i-Aam. The thirty-six closely vaulted and pendulous brackets, which are supported by a circular platform leads into four passages called the Diwan-i-Khas. It is here that Akbar held his religious discourses.

Panch Mahal

Panch Mahal stands on the western line of the courtyard. It is a five-storeyed pavilion which served as the badgir—a tower meant for the ladies. One hundred and seventy-six differently carved pillars support this tower. These screens acted as purdah for the queens and the princesses when they spent time on the terrace enjoying the cool wind.

Jami Masjid

Jami Masjid was built in 1571—the first structure to be built in Sikri. Akbar was emotionally attached to this mosque and it is believed that he occasionally swept the floor and gave the call to prayer from this mosque. This mosque has a modest exterior and an intricately designed interior. The interior of the mosque has the finest ornamentation in floral arabesques and geometrical patterns in black, white, brown, red and turquoise. The spacious courtyard had the capacity to accommodate ten thousand men at a time. This Masjid adds a stately charm to the whole place.

Buland Darwaza

In 1575, Akbar built the Buland Darwaza on the southern wall of the courtyard. This colossal triumphal arch was built to celebrate his conquest of Gujarat. This towering gateway spans a height of 176 feet above ground level and 134 feet over the top step. This magnificent structure contains modest ornamentation with a famous line inscribed on it, 'The world is but a bridge: Pass over but build no houses on it.' The glorious central arch is considered to be the most magnificent structure in the entire range of Mughal architecture in India.

Palaces in the harem

Akbar, had a large entourage of queens, princesses, and other women companions in his harem. To house these women, Akbar built the Haresara—female quarters—in the largest central area in the royal enclosure at Sikri. He divided the harems among his women according to their position.

Jodhabai, his chief queen, lived in the largest palace called the Harkha. She shared the palace with the other Rajput wives from Bikaner, Marwar, Jaisalmer, Merta and Durgapur. This high-walled edifice was guarded by a grand gateway that led to a spectacular courtyard. The colonnade pattern on all four sides of the double storeyed pavilions resembled Hindu architectural features. Hindu motifs such as swans, parrots, elephants and the Srivatsa mark decorated the interior of the building.

Hamida Begum, Akbar's mother, lived in a smaller palace called the Sunehra Makan. This palace was also called the golden house because of the golden paint on the faded murals that lined the walls.

The third palace in the harem quarters was called Birbal Mahal. It belonged to Akbar's two senior wives—Ruqayya Sultan Begum and Salima Sultan Begum. Salima Begum was Bairam Khan's widow who married Akbar. Birbal's daughter was also married to Akbar and later shared this palace with the other two women. This could be why the palace is named after Birbal.

Tomb of Sheikh Salim Chisti

Sheikh Salim Chisti was a famous Sufi saint and the descendant of Khawaja Moinuddin Chisti, the most famous Sufi saint of the Chisti Order. He is the most outstanding figure in the annals of Islamic mysticism and was the founder of the Chistiya order in India. He established this order in Ajmer and became popular during Akbar's reign.

Salim Chisti was highly revered in Akbar's court. Legend says that Akbar sought the blessing of this Sufi to beget a son. When his wish was fulfilled, Akbar named his son 'Salim' after this saint. This son was none other than the future emperor Jahangir, In 1580, years after the death of this saint, Akbar built a tomb in his remembrance. It was made of pure red sandstone. The tomb has beautifully carved marble stones with finely designed jali screens. It displays a rare perfection of craftsmanship. The wide chajja on all four sides of the edifice is supported by serpentine brackets that add grace to the whole structure.

Akbar's tomb at Sikandra

Akbar started the construction of his tomb a few years before his death in 1605. It was his son Jahangir who finished it after his death. Located 4 km from Agra, Sikandra is a quaint little town where Akbar's tomb stands today. This structure resembles different styles of architecture and is very different from the other Mughal buildings. It also carries the flavour of the tiered pavilion of the Agra fort and Fatehpur Sikri. Its muddled style is probably because it was started by one person and completed by another.

The tomb is housed in a large walled garden on the Delhi-Agra road. It can be entered through an elegant southern gateway that leads to an enclosed garden. The gateway is covered with floral and geometrical arabesque decorations done in white and coloured marble. The stateliness of this gateway makes it the most magnificent entrance to any monument in the country. The four gardens lead to the pyramidal structure of Akbar's Tomb, which is a bright red-tiered structure that resembles a castle of playing cards.

Tomb of Sheikh Salim Chisti

The building has five levels. The first is a podium of arches. An inlaid framed door faces each podium. The other three levels are made of red sandstone and are flat roofed and supported by a row of pillars. The verandah on all four sides is crafted by large panels of jali screens. Akbar's grave lies interred in the basement that can be entered through the portico which is adorned with stucco paintings in gold, blue and green floral arabesque of Persian inscriptions. Akbar's aesthetic sense was at its peak when he designed the edifice at Sikandra.

Shah Jahan, who built the world's monumental beauty—the Taj Mahal, seemed to have inherited his grandfather Akbar's architectural skills.

Akbar's Nine Gems

Akbar enjoyed the intellectual debates on religious issues in the Ibadat Khana and revelled in the company of the most learned men in his court. Like the courts of many Indian rulers, Akbar's court also consisted of navaratnas—a group of nine extraordinary men who excelled in the fields of education, arts and spirituality. These men were known as the jewels of Akbar's court. The nine gems of Akbar's court were:

Abul-Fazl

Abul-Fazl served as vizier in the Mughal court. He is better known as the author of the official history of Akbar's reign titled *Akbarnama*. He held liberal views on religion and influenced Akbar to a great extent. Abu-Fazl was among the few nobles who opposed the accession of Jahangir to the throne. The angry prince killed him in 1602 as a punishment for his opposition.

Faizi

Faizi, the poet laureate of Akbar's court, is known for his *Nal u Daman*—a poetic rendering of the story of Nala and Damayanti.

His command over Persian was very strong and he rendered over 100 poems in Persian. Akbar realised the genius in him and appointed him as his son's teacher.

Raja Todar Mal

Raja Todar Mal, born in Laharpur, Oudh, was the finance minister of the Mughal court. Being from the Kayastha community, Todar Mal was excellent with land revenue systems and land reform policies. He incorporated successful agricultural policies during his tenure. Apart from being a good finance minister and land revenue officer, he was also a good warrior. He assisted Akbar in controlling the Afghan rebels in Bengal.

Raja Man Singh

Raja Man Singh, also called Kunwar Man Singh, was the Raja of Amber, the present-day Jaipur. He was a trusted general in Akbar's court. He was a devotee of Lord Krishna and did not follow Akbar's Din-i-Ilahi. He was known in Akbar's court for his courage and valour. He fought many battles for Akbar, the most important being the Battle of Haldighati.

Akbar sent Raja Man Singh to fight Rana Pratap, who had refused to accept the Mughal sovereignty. On 18 June 1576, a battle ensued between Rana Pratap and Raja Man Singh at Haldighati. Rana Pratap was no match for Man Singh's power. He had to flee from the battle ground to save his life. Raja Man Singh helped Akbar win many battles. In 1580, he led an army against Mirza Hakim in Kabul. Man Singh dared to enter the swelling

Indus River and seeing this his jittery opponent surrendered to Akbar.

In 1585, Raja Man Singh was asked by Akbar to help Raja Todar Mal in fighting against the rebellious Afghan tribes. Raja Man Singh defeated five major tribes of Afghans. This included the 'Yusufzai' and 'Mandar' tribes, the most powerful of the Afghan tribes.

In 1588, Raja Man Singh, the Governor of Bihar, led an army against Katlu Shah of Orissa. Raja Man Singh won the battle easily and appointed Nisar Khan, Katlu Shah's son as the Governor of Orissa. Nisar Khan remained faithful to the Mughals only for a short while. To crush the uprising, Raja Man Singh again led an army against Orissa in 1592 and won the battle.

Akbar made him the Governor of Bengal, Bihar and Orissa in 1594. During his service as a Governor, Man Singh expanded the Mughal territory by fighting many battles. Akbar was very fond of Raja Man Singh and regarded him as his son.

Abdul Rahim Khan-i-Khana

Abdul Rahim Khan, better known as Rahim, was an important noble and a renowned poet in Persian, Sanskrit, and Hindustani. He was the son of Akbar's general, Bairam Khan. Akbar married Bairam Khan's widow which made Rahim his stepson.

Rahim held a high place among the nine gems. Rahim was born a Muslim, but he was a devotee of Lord Krishna. He wrote many dohas and poems in praise of the lord Krishna. Apart from this, he translated Babur's memoirs from Turkish to Persian. His command over Sanskrit was outstanding. He also wrote two books on Astrology titled *Kheta Kautukama* and *Dwawishad Yogavali.* Rahim was a kind-hearted and generous man. He helped the needy in many ways. It is believed that he never made eye contact with the person who was receiving alms from him. Such was his humility.

Fakir Aziao-Din

Fakir Aziao Din was one of Akbar's chief advisors. 'Fakir' means 'sage' or 'ascetic' in Urdu. As his name suggests, he was sought after for his wise counsel and was highly respected in Akbar's court.

Mullah Do Piaza

Mullah Do Piaza served as one of Akbar's chief advisors. Mullah Do Piaza was known for his smartness. He was so smart that he even outfoxed Birbal. Akbar, was highly amused with their clashes and would encourage Mullah Do Piaza and Birbal to parry wits in court. Mullah was held in high esteem by Akbar.

Mian Tansen

Mian Tansen was one of the greatest musicians of all times. He was instrumental in creating the classical style of north Indian music as we know it today. Tansen was born to a Hindu family in Gwalior. He came from a family of poets and singers. He converted to Islam at the hands of the great Sufi saint, Shaykh Muhammad Ghaus. Next to his tomb is a tamarind tree and it is believed that a leaf eaten from this tree will improve a singer's voice.

Tansen's music is an undying legacy in India. Even today, many famous musicians follow the style he created.

Tansen was born to the wealthy poet, Makrand Ram Pandey and his wife with the blessings of the saint and musician, Muhammad Ghaus. Pandey provided the best of education to his son. However, Tansen seemed more interested in learning the sounds of birds and animals in the nearby forest.

Once Tansen roared like a tiger and scared a group of singers who were passing through the forest. He appeared in front of them and impressed with his mimicry, the leader encouraged Tansen to display his talent. The leader of that group was so pleased with Tansen that he immediately wanted to take him on as his disciple. The leader was none other than the great musician and poet, Haridas.

Tansen's parents agreed to send him and for the next ten years, he studied music under Haridas in Brindavan. Starting with the basic notes, Tansen learnt to sing and play the tanpura. He learnt the importance of each raga and mastered them all. He learnt the ragas which depicted the different moods of human nature.

Tansen had to leave for his village when his father was on his deathbed. Before his death, Pandey asked his son to meet Muhammad Ghaus and accordingly after the death of his parents, Tansen with the permission of his guru Haridas went to see Muhammad Ghaus.

Tansen studied under the Sufi saint for three years and developed his musical talents. During this period he was introduced to the king of Gwalior.

After the death of Ghaus, Tansen became the court musician of Rewa, near Gwalior. This was Tansen's first step to becoming a great musician.

Tansen's fame grew to a great measure in the court of Rewa. Akbar heard Tansen's music on a visit to Rewa and was so impressed that he requested the king of Rewa to send Tansen to his court. Reluctantly, Tansen was sent to the Mughal court.

Akbar overwhelmed by the magic created by Tansen's music bestowed upon him the greatest honour of his court. He became one of the nine gems of Akbar's court. Tansen's excellence in music spread far and wide. It was said that he was capable of taming even the wildest of animals in the forest with the power of his music.

Birbal

Birbal, a poor Brahmin by birth, was a noble in the Mughal court. Birbal's duties were mostly military and administrative, but he was Akbar's most trusted and intimate friend. Birbal was famous for his wit and wisdom.

Once, during a hunt, Akbar and his soldiers lost their way to the city. They wandered for a long time and came to a cross section of roads. They stood there wondering which road to take when a young boy came that way. Akbar asked him which of those roads went to Agra. The lad was quick to answer that the road could not go anywhere.

Akbar was amused by the boy's witty remark and rephrased his question. The boy pointed the right direction to Agra. He then introduced himself as Mahesh Das. Akbar presented his ring to Mahesh Das and asked him to come to his court.

A few days later, Birbal went to meet Akbar in Agra. He was stopped at the gate by Akbar's guard. Birbal explained the reason for his visit, but the guard did not budge. Finally, when Birbal showed the guard the Emperor's ring, the guard realised his mistake. However he let Birbal go only after extracting a promise to share half the reward he received from the king.

In Akbar's court Birbal was welcomed warmly. Akbar offered several gifts to him, but he only asked for 100 whip lashes. The stunned Emperor tried to talk him out of his stupidity. In the end, Akbar gave in to Birbal's strange request and half-heartedly asked his men to whip Birbal. Birbal then asked for the gatekeeper to be sent in to share the reward with him. On learning the entire story, Akbar had a hearty laugh. Impressed with his smartness, Akbar immediately appointed Birbal to his court and also made him a part of his nine gems.

These nine gems were the soul of Akbar's court. Akbar took their counsel for all important political issues. He held them in high esteem and honoured them lavishly with titles and gifts.

The Mughals after Akbar

Akbar was undoubtedly the most successful Mughal emperor. However, in his personal life he suffered greatly—in his early years he was tortured by his cruel uncle and in his last years the misconduct of his sons pained him. Of his four sons, Akbar lost two of them to alcohol. His third son, Salim—named after the Sufi saint Salim Chisti—was in constant rebellion against him. Excessive personal stress showed on his health and Akbar was soon bedridden.

Akbar was succeeded by his favourite son Salim, who later became Emperor Jahangir. Nuruddin Salim Jahangir (1569 – 1627) took more after his grandfather, Humayun and his great grandfather, Babur than his father, Akbar.

Akbar was uneducated, but he was involved in great literary activities during his reign. He provided the best form of education to all his children. Jahangir's education commenced at the age of four and he was trained in Persian, Turkish,

Arabic, Urdu, history, arithmetic, geography and other sciences. Jahangir turned out to be a good writer and a lover of nature. He recorded the wild tales of his life in his autobiography *Tuzk-e-Jahangiri*. Under his rule, the courtly culture of the Mughals flourished. Mughal paintings and other forms of art reached its zenith during this period.

As a king, Jahangir expanded the Mughal Empire to a considerable extent. He won many battles and crushed various rebellions. Jahangir believed in protecting his religion and restored the Islamic faith in his provinces. His famous 'chain of justice' brought him closer to his subjects. The chain was a link between him and his people. Any man could ring this bell and gain a personal meeting with the king.

In spite of his merits, Jahangir fell an easy prey to flattery. He was easy to influence and was exploited by many due to this. This was one of the main reasons why his wife, Nur Jahan, was able to actively participate in the administration of the kingdom.

Jahangir was succeeded by his son, Shah Jahan, in 1627. He exhibited a rare degree of centralised control of the state. Like Akbar, Shah Jahan was highly talented and his architectural prowess has given India its most exquisite edifice—the Taj Mahal.

In 1658, Aurangzeb succeeded Shah Jahan. He did away with the policies brought in by his great grandfather, Akbar, and was known by many as a Muslim fanatic and bigot. Aurangzeb eventually lost the far-flung Mughal Empire because of his unpopularity with his subjects.

Mughal Achievements

- Consolidation of Islam in South Asia. They spread Muslim—particularly Persian—arts and culture along with its religious faith.
- Hindus were given equal opportunity in the Mughal courts, especially during Akbar's reign.
- They formulated a centralised form of government by bringing many small kingdoms together.
- Human rights were given prime importance and government bodies were delegated accordingly.
- They exhibited great military skills.
- Trade routes and trade systems flourished during the Mughal era.
- Persian art and culture fused with Indian art and culture.
- Persian language combined with Arabic and Hindi to create Urdu, one of the official languages in India today.
- Great religious tolerance was practiced during Akbar's time.
- Architectural excellence was achieved.

An educational system was designed to cater to the needs of the pupils' culture.

Important Dates

1542	15 October Akbar is born in Sindh
1543	Akbar is left with his uncle Askari in Afghanistan
1550	Akbar is re-united with his parents
1556	Akbar reaches Sirhind to take over the Punjab; Humayun dies and Akbar is coronated; The Second Battle of Panipat – against Hemu
1558	Akbar re-entered Delhi
1560	Akbar takes complete control over his kingdom; Bairam Khan dies
1562	Fall of Merat
1564	Allahabad is conquered; Abolished the pilgrim tax
1565	Battle of Talikota; Abolished the Jizyah tax
1566	Akbar returns to Agra
1567	Lahore conquered
1568	Fall of Chittoor
1569	Jahangir, Akbar's son and successor is born
1571	Jami Masjid built—first structure to be built in Fatehpur Sikri
1572	Akbar wins Gujarat

1573 Surat is taken over

1575 Battle of Tukaroi; Buland Darwaza built in Sikri

1576 Battle of Haldighat – against Rana Pratap

1577 Akbar invades Kandesh

1580 Seized Bihar and Bengal from Ibrahim Adil Shah II; Tomb of Salim Chisti built in Sikri

1581 Akbar defeats Muhammad Hakim

1582 Prince Daniel and prince Murad die of excessive drinking

1584 Jahangir's marriage celebrated in Fatehpur Sikri

1586 Kashmir captured

1587 Srinagar is won

1591 Conquest of Sind

1592 Orissa captured

1594 Raja Man Singh made governor of Bengal, Bihar and Orissa

1595 Siege of Ahmednagar; Annexation of Baluchistan

1597 Akbar completes his conquest

1601 Akbar settles in Agra; Begins the construction of Akbar's tomb at Sikandra

1602 Jahangir kills Abul Fazl

1605 Akbar dies